KETO DRINKS

Tasty Ketogenic Cocktails, Warm Drinks and Lemonades for Weight Loss

The Collection of Low-Carb Recipes

That Will Keep You In Ketosis

Emma Green

CONTENTS

INTRODUCTION

U p to 80% of our body is water. So technically, we are just restless cucumbers. But we still need to drink water, and not only water, but low carb nutritious drinks. When it comes to drinks on keto, plain old water is the king. Both still and sparkling.

The book offers a collection of 55 beverages —non-alcoholic cocktails, lemonades, warm drinks, and alcoholic cocktails allowed on a low-carb diet.

Always keep your organism well hydrated. In the first few days of limiting carbs, the body loses water and minerals at double the speed. To prevent dehydration, consume a lot of water and minerals every day. It is crucial, not only in those early days but for however long you stay on the ketogenic diet, that you always take special care to drink enough water and add enough salt to your diet, as much as 3500-5000 mg of sodium per day. You can make "keto-water" by adding 1/8 tsp salt to 1 liter of water and drinking it on a regular basis. Two liters of keto-water a day will be sufficient for most people.

Please pay close attention to the warm drinks section. Most of the herbal teas have zero carbs and tremendous healthy effects—for example mint has a calming effect, while cilantro is a source of dietary fiber and also contains vitamins A, E, K, and rosehip can boost vitamin C.

What is Keto?

The ketogenic diet is a low carbohydrate, high fat, and moderate protein diet that puts the body into a metabolic state called ketosis. It diet involves radically reducing carbohydrate intake and substituting it with fat.

When your foods are high in carbs, your body will produce glucose and insulin.

- Glucose is an energy source that is the easiest for our bodies to convert into energy and use. Thus, it will be chosen over any other energy source.
- Insulin is a hormone that processes the glucose so that your bloodstream can distribute it around your body.

Since glucose is the main form of energy, fats are not used and are, therefore, stored. Typically, on a normal, higher carbohydrate diet, the body will use glucose as its primary energy source. But due to the incredible adaptive abilities of our bodies, we can induce it into a state known as ketosis by lowering the intake of carbs.

Ketosis is a natural process the body uses to help us survive when food intake is low. During this state, chemicals called ketones are produced. This process is started not by a lack of calories, but by a lack of carbohydrates.

Vegetables & Fruits on Keto

Here is a quick reminder of the best keto-friendly fruits and vegetables with their carb count per 100g:
- Spinach (1.43g)
- Kale (5.15g)
- Broccoli (4.01g)
- Collard Greens (1.40g)
- Swiss Chard (2.14g)
- Arugula (2.05g)
- Romaine (1.19g)
- Butter head (1.10g)
- Watercress (0.79g)
- Cauliflower (2.97g)
- Broccoli (4.40g)
- Radishes (1.80g)
- White cabbage (3.07g)
- Green cabbage (3.00g)
- Bok choy (1.18g)
- Brussels sprouts (5.15g)
- Kale (5.15g)
- Zucchini (2.11g)
- Cucumbers (3.13g)
- Avocado (1.84g)
- Green beans (4.27g)
- Sauerkraut (great when naturally fermented, but beware of low-quality brands and added sugar — 4.28g)

- Turnips (4.63g)
- Bamboo shoots (3.00g)
- Asparagus (1.78g)
- Summer squash (2.25g)
- Celery (1.37g)
- Artichoke hearts (3.88g)
- Eggplant (2.88g)
- Bell peppers (2.9g)
- Okra (4.25g)
- Garlic (0.99g in one clove)

This doesn't necessarily mean other vegetables are forbidden, most of them just are to be consumed in moderation. Typically, the more brightly colored, the higher chance they contain more carbs. It is really recommended to avoid starchy vegetables like potatoes, parsnips, green peas, corn, and leeks.

- Starfruit (3.93g)
- Blackberry (4.31g)
- Raspberry (5.44g)
- Strawberry (5.68g)
- Honeydew Melon (5.68g)
- Coconut Meat (6.23g)
- Lemon (6.52g)
- Watermelon (7.15 g)
- Cantaloupe (7.26g)
- Peach (8.05g)
- Cranberry (8.37g)
- Apricot (9.12g)
- Plum (10.02g)
- Granny Smith Apple (10.81g)
- Kiwi (11.6g)
- Blueberry (12.09g)

Spices in Mixed Drinks

Using herbs and spices in cocktails is not new. Spices can enhance any drink and give you an unforgettable taste. Here is a tip on how to mix spices to get the most out of them:

- Cilantro: Pair with ginger, chili peppers, figs, cucumbers, cumin seed
- Basil: Pair with strawberries, cucumbers, orange peel, peaches, pineapple
- Lemon Verbena: Pair with blueberries, cherries, cinnamon, currants
- Tarragon: Pair with lemon thyme, celery, lemon, pink grapefruit
- Dill: Pair with cucumber, coriander, cilantro, capers, lemon
- Mint: Pair with apples, cardamom, whole cloves, grapes, peaches
- Rosemary: Pair with lemon, orange slices, apricots, plums
- Thyme: Pair with allspice, bay leaf, celery, cranberries, sage
- Lavender: Pair with raspberries, blackberries, strawberries, lemon

Everyday Drinks

Water. Mineral or spring water is okay since it has no carbs.

Coffee. Coffee with no sugar added is okay. You may add any non-dairy milk or even 1 tbsp of low fat cow's milk.

Tea. Black, green, or herbal tea with no sugar added is okay.

Sugar-free sodas. Make your own using sparkling water or opt for natural ones with no sugar added.

Non-dairy milk. Use nut milks that are unsweetened.

Alcohol Cheat List

On a keto diet, you can still enjoy a delicious alcoholic drink or two on special occasions. Even though many alcoholic drinks contain a lot of sugar, there are still some really good options with little carbs.

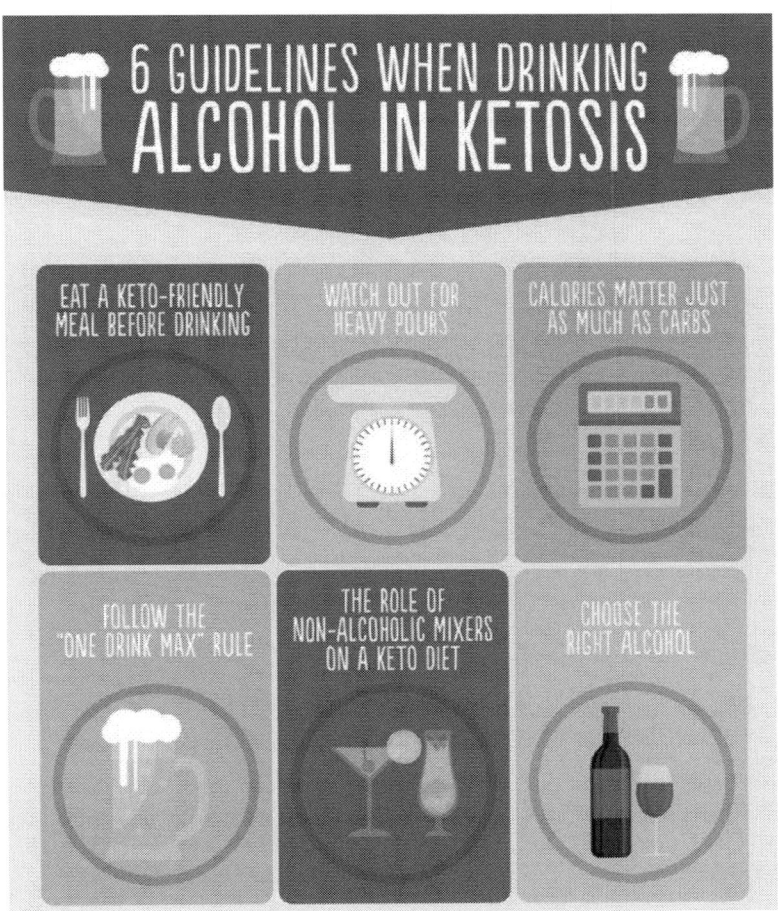

Acceptable alcohol includes:

- Vodka
- Whiskey
- Rum
- Scotch
- Brandy
- Cognac
- Tequila
- Gin

- Champagne
- Wine

Below is the visual guide of alcoholic drinks with the number of carb grams per serving:

Spirits

Whiskey **0**

Dry Martini **0**

Brandy **0**

Bloody Mary **7**

Cosmopolitan **13**

White Russian **17**

Rum & Coke **39**

Tequila shot **0**

Vodka & soda water **0**
aka "Skinny Bitch"

Margarita **8**

Gin & Tonic **16**

Vodka & orange juice **28**

Fewer carbs ⟵

More carbs ⟶

Wine and beer

Champagne **1**

Red wine **2**

White wine **2**

Beer **13**

Fewer carbs ⟵

More carbs ⟶

Serving Sizes of Glassware

Each beverage has its own serving glass with a certain capacity. Here is a short guide:

Wineglass (White wine)

A glass on a stemmed base, usually about 4 oz.

Wineglass (Red wine)

A glass for red wine is typically a little taller and larger than the one for white wine. It makes 4 or 5 oz and allows the wine to bring out its full flavor.

Champagne glass

Tall flute or tulip glass is a glass for sparkling wines and cocktail with them. A 4 to 10 oz bowl won't affect the temperature.

Brandy Snifter

A snifter, or cognac glass, has a wide-bottom bowl and short stemmed base.

Short Tumbler

A 5 or 6 oz capacity tumbler with weighted bottom is used for many types of drinks – from water and fruit juices to whiskey on the rocks and Old Fashioned.

Tall Tumbler

A 10 to 12 oz capacity tumbler with narrow body is perfect for cocktails mixed with juiced, iced tea, highballs, and other drinks with lots of ice.

Cocktail Glass

A 4 oz cocktail for straight-up cocktails, martinis, and Manhattans.

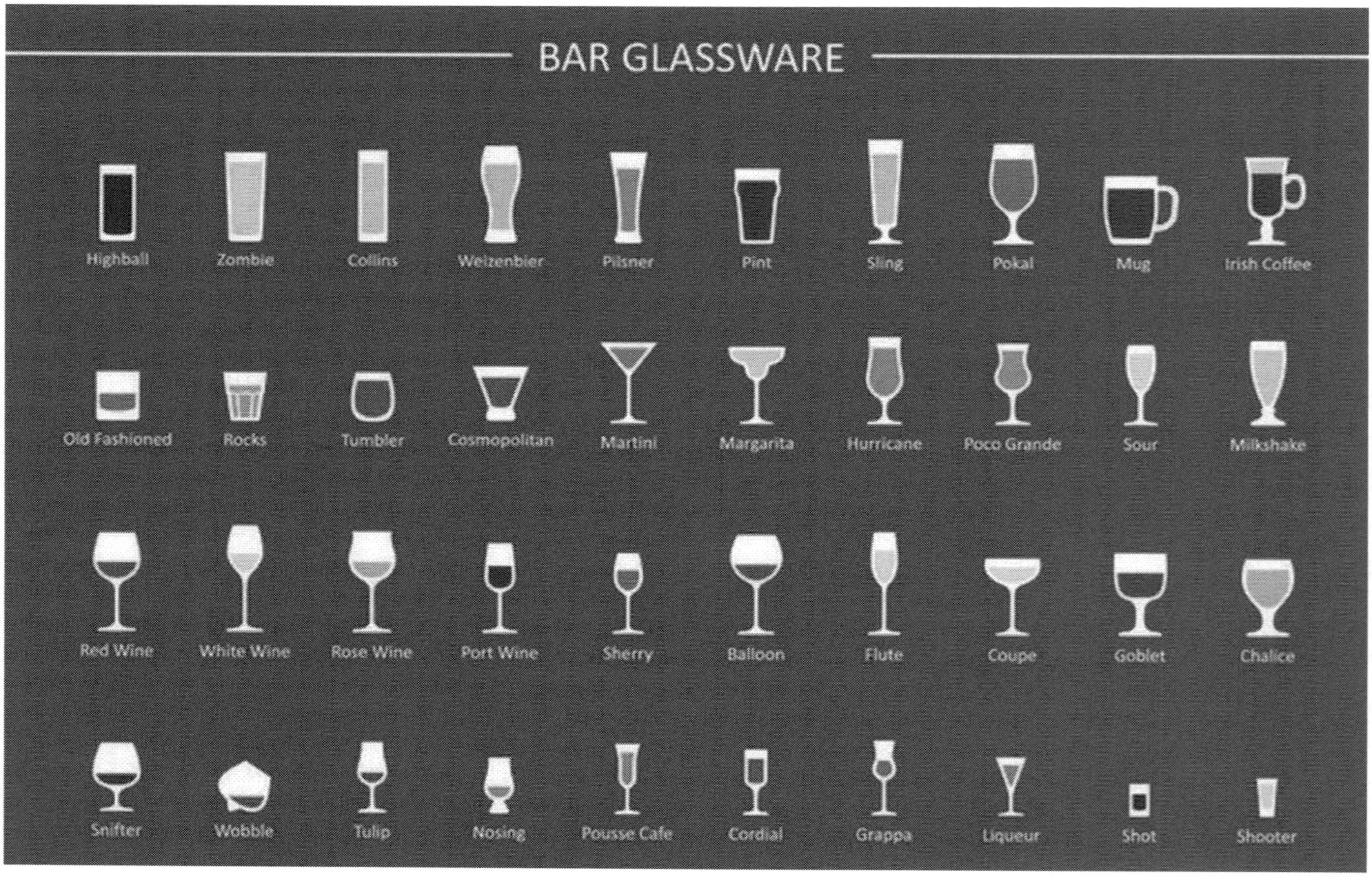

BAR GLASSWARE

Highball	Zombie	Collins	Weizenbier	Pilsner	Pint	Sling	Pokal	Mug	Irish Coffee
Old Fashioned	Rocks	Tumbler	Cosmopolitan	Martini	Margarita	Hurricane	Poco Grande	Sour	Milkshake
Red Wine	White Wine	Rose Wine	Port Wine	Sherry	Balloon	Flute	Coupe	Goblet	Chalice
Snifter	Wobble	Tulip	Nosing	Pousse Cafe	Cordial	Grappa	Liqueur	Shot	Shooter

Cocktails

Turmeric Cocktail

Prep time: 1 minute

Cooking time: 0 minutes

Servings: 1

Nutrients per serving:

Total Carbs – 6 g

Fat – 10 g

Protein –1 g

Calories – 118

Ingredients:

- ½ cup whey
- 1 tsp turmeric powder
- ½ Tbsp flaxseed oil
- ½ cup water
- ½ cup tomato juice
- Dash of black pepper

Instructions:

1. Combine all ingredients in a blender and pulse on high.
2. Serve.

Sorrel Cocktail

Prep time: 3 minutes

Cooking time: 0 minutes

Servings: 4

Nutrients per serving:

Total Carbs – 27 g

Fat – 0.6 g

Protein – 2 g

Calories – 127

Ingredients:

- 1 medium bunch of sorrel, rinsed
- ¼ cup spinach, rinsed
- ½ whole pineapple, peeled, cored, cubed
- 2 oranges, juiced
- ½ lime, juiced

Instructions:

1. Combine all ingredients in a blender and pulse on high.
2. Serve.

Sorrel & Apple Cocktail

Prep time: 3 minutes

Cooking time: 0 minutes

Servings: 2

Nutrients per serving:

Total Carbs – 41 g

Fat – 0.8 g

Protein – 2.3 g

Calories – 166

Ingredients:

- 4 green apples, juiced
- 1 orange, peeled, quartered
- 1 medium bunch sorrel, rinsed

Instructions:

1. Combine all ingredients in a blender and pulse on high.
2. Serve.

Walnut milkshake

Prep time: 8hours 2 minutes

Cooking time: 0 minutes

Servings: 3

Nutrients per serving:

Total Carbs – 18 g

Fat – 26 g

Protein – 6.8 g

Calories – 323

Ingredients:

- 3 cups cold water, divided
- 1 cup walnuts, soaked overnight
- 1 banana, chopped
- 2 Tbsp oats
- 1 Tbsp vanilla extract
- 1 tsp honey

Instructions:

1. Put the walnuts into a blender with 1 cup of water and blend. Add remaining water and blend well.
2. Add the remaining ingredients and pulse on high.

Avocado & Berry Cocktail

Prep time: 1 minute

Cooking time: 0 minutes

Servings: 2

Nutrients per serving:

Total Carbs – 20.9 g

Fat – 7.2 g

Protein – 2.7 g

Calories – 144

Ingredients:

- 2 cups water
- 2 cups spinach
- 1 cup blueberries
- 1 kiwi
- ½ avocado

Instructions:

1. Combine spinach and water in a blender and pulse on high.
2. Add the remaining ingredients and blend until smooth.

Parsley Cocktail

Prep time: 1 minute

Cooking time: 0 minutes

Servings: 1

Nutrients per serving:

Total Carbs – 23 g

Fat – 0.6 g

Protein – 2.2 g

Calories – 94

Ingredients:

- 1 cup parsley leaves, rinsed
- ½ lemon, peeled, seedless, cut into pieces
- 1 Tbsp honey
- 1 1/4 cup water

Instructions:

1. Add all ingredients to a blender and pulse on high until smooth.
2. Serve.

Melon Fresh Minting Cocktail

Prep time: 3 minutes

Cooking time: 0 minute

Servings: 2

Nutrients per serving:

Total Carbs – 31 g

Fat – 1 g

Protein – 3.3 g

Calories – 122

Ingredients:

- 2 cups honeydew melon flesh
- 1 ½ cups kiwi flesh
- 10 mint leaves
- 1 Tbsp lemon juice
- 2 cups crushed ice
- 1 tsp stevia

Instructions:

1. Add all ingredients to a blender and pulse on high until smooth.
2. Serve.

Cranberry Cocktail

Prep time: 1 minute

Cooking time: 0 minutes

Servings: 2

Nutrients per serving:

Total Carbs – 16 g

Fat – 0.2 g

Protein – 0.1 g

Calories – 72

Ingredients:

- 1 cup cranberries
- 1 cup apple juice
- 1 cup water

Instructions:

1. Add all ingredients to a blender and pulse on high until smooth.
2. Serve.

Multi vegetables Cocktail

Prep time: 3 minutes

Cooking time: 0 minutes

Servings: 2

Nutrients per serving:

Total Carbs – 13 g

Fat – 0.2 g

Protein – 2.8 g

Calories – 57

Ingredients:

- 1 bell pepper, deseeded, cored, sliced
- 1 bunch of spinach, rinsed
- 2 cups tomato juice
- Dash of black pepper
- Dash of salt

Instructions:

1. Add all ingredients to a blender and pulse on high until smooth.
2. Serve.

Ginger Cocktail

Prep time: 3 minutes

Cooking time: 0 minutes

Servings: 1

Nutrients per serving:

Total Carbs – 17 g

Fat – 8 g

Protein – 8.2 g

Calories – 171

Ingredients:

- 1 cup kefir, low fat
- 2 tsp ginger root, grated
- 1 tsp cinnamon
- Dash of red hot pepper

Instructions:

1. Add all ingredients to a blender and pulse on high until smooth.
2. Serve.

Rhubarb Cocktail

Prep time: 3 minutes

Cooking time: 0 minutes

Servings: 1-2

Nutrients per serving:

Total Carbs – 26 g

Fat – 0.5 g

Protein – 1.8 g

Calories – 108

Ingredients:

- 1/3 whole pineapple, peeled, cored
- 2 rhubarb stalks, peeled, cut in pieces
- 1 cup orange juice
- Fresh mint leaves, to taste (2-4 leaves)

Instructions:

1. Add all ingredients to a blender and pulse on high until smooth.
2. Serve.

Cacao Cherry Shake

Prep time: 3 minutes

Cooking time: 0 minutes

Servings: 2

Nutrients per serving:

Total Carbs – 28 g

Fat – 61.2 g

Protein – 10 g

Calories – 625

Ingredients:

- 2 cups coconut milk
- ½ cup cherries, pitted
- 4 tsp cacao powder
- 2 tsp stevia powder

Instructions:

1. Add all ingredients to a blender and pulse on high until smooth.
2. Serve.

Cold Chocolate

Prep time: 3 minutes

Cooking time: 0 minutes

Servings: 3

Nutrients per serving:

Total Carbs – 13.9 g

Fat – 7.7 g

Protein – 5.7 g

Calories – 90

Ingredients:

- 1 cup freshly brewed coffee, cooled
- 4 Tbsp cacao powder
- 2 Tbsp coconut milk
- 15 ice cubes
- 2-3 tsp sweetener

Instructions:

1. Add all ingredients to a blender and pulse on high until smooth.
2. Serve.

Harsh Tomato

Prep time: 2 minutes

Cooking time: 0 minutes

Servings: 1

Nutrients per serving:

Total Carbs – 11.8g

Fat – 0.4 g

Protein – 2.3 g

Calories – 52

Ingredients:

- 1 cup tomato juice (with salt)
- 1 ½ tbsp lemon juice
- 2 small celery stalks, cut
- 3 drops Tabasco
- Ice, to taste (usually the ice covers more than half the glass)

Instructions:

1. Add all ingredients to a blender and pulse on high until smooth.
2. Serve.

Lemonades

Classical Lemonade

Prep time: 5 minutes

Cooking time: 0 minutes

Servings: 7 cups

Nutrients per serving:

Total Carbs – 2 g

Fat –0 g

Protein – 0 g

Calories – 7

Ingredients:

- 1 cup lemon juice
- 6 cups water
- 1 tsp liquid stevia
- Ice, to taste (usually the ice covers more than half the glass)

Instructions:

1. Combine all ingredients in a blender.
2. Serve.

Basil & Mint Lemonade

Prep time: 2 hours

Cooking time: 0 minutes

Servings: 2

Nutrients per serving:

Total Carbs – 2.5 g

Fat – 0.4 g

Protein – 1.3 g

Calories – 24

Ingredients:

- 1 bunch basil
- 1 bunch mint
- 2 lemons, juiced
- 4 cups water
- 1 tsp liquid stevia extract

Instructions:

1. Combine water with lemon juice.
2. Add basil and mint leaves to a blender and pulse.
3. Add the blended leaves to lemon water and let stand for 2 hours covered.
4. Filter the lemonade, leaving the leaves behind.
5. Stir in stevia and serve.

Cucumber Lemonade

Prep time: 2 minutes

Cooking time: 0 minutes

Servings: 1

Nutrients per serving:

Total Carbs – 15 g

Fat – 0.3 g

Protein – 1.2 g

Calories – 90

Ingredients:

- 1 cucumber, cut in chunks
- ½ lime, juiced
- ½ orange, juiced
- 2 sprigs rosemary
- 1 tsp honey
- 1 cup water

Instructions:

1. Combine all ingredients in a blender and pulse on high.
2. Serve.

Lettuce leaves Lemonade

Prep time: 3 minutes

Cooking time: 0 minutes

Servings: 2

Nutrients per serving:

Total Carbs – 8.8 g

Fat – 0 g

Protein – 2.4 g

Calories – 36

Ingredients:

- 4 lettuce leaves, rinsed, torn
- ½ cup mint leaves, rinsed
- 1 lemon, juiced + zest
- 2 cups water
- 10 ice cubes
- ½ tsp stevia extract

Instructions:

1. Combine all ingredients and pulse on high.
2. Add ice cubes and serve.

Green Tea Lemonade

Prep time: 2 minutes + 1-2 hours in the fridge

Cooking time: 0 minutes

Servings: 4

Nutrients per serving:

Total Carbs – 3.3 g

Fat – 0.1 g

Protein – 1.1 g

Calories – 18

Ingredients:

- 4 cups green tea
- 3 lemons, juiced
- 1 bunch mint leaves, rinsed
- 1 cup water

Instructions:

1. Combine all ingredients in a jar and put into the fridge until cooled.
2. Serve.

Lavender Lemonade

Prep time: 1 hour 10 minutes + 1-2 hours to cool

Cooking time: 5 minutes

Servings: 4

Nutrients per serving:

Total Carbs – 5.4 g

Fat – 0.3 g

Protein – 0.6 g

Calories – 19

Ingredients:

- 2 tbsp dried lavender
- 3 lemons, juiced
- 4 ½ cups water
- 1/3 stevia extract, liquid

Instructions:

1. Add 2 1/2 cups of water into a skillet and bring to boil. Reduce the heat and simmer for 5 minutes. Remove from heat and let stand for 1 hour covered.
2. Filter out the lavender flowers, and add lemon juice, water, and stevia.
3. Pour the lemonade into a jar and place into the fridge to cool.

Pear Lemonade with Sage

Prep time: 3 minutes

Cooking time: 0 minutes

Servings: 1

Nutrients per serving:

Total Carbs – 12.2 g

Fat – 0.3 g

Protein – 0.8 g

Calories – 52

Ingredients:

- 1 Tbsp fresh sage leaves
- ½ lime, sliced
- ¼ cup sparkling water
- ½ cup pear juice
- Crushed ice

Instructions:

1. Put lime slice and sage leaves into a tumbler.
2. Add a couple of tablespoons of crushed ice.
3. Pour in the pear juice and sparkling water.
4. Decorate with sage leaf or lime slice.

Green Lemonade

Prep time: 7 minutes

Cooking time: 0 minutes

Servings: 2

Nutrients per serving:

Total Carbs – 13 g

Fat – 1 g

Protein – 3.4 g

Calories – 66

Ingredients:

- 4 cucumbers
- 4 celery stalks
- 1 lemon
- 1 cup collard greens
- 1 cup water

Instructions:

1. Juice all ingredients and combine the juices with water.
2. Serve cool.

Basil Lemonade

Prep time: 3 minutes + 1 hour to cool in the fridge

Cooking time: 0 minutes

Servings: 3

Nutrients per serving:

Total Carbs – 16.5 g

Fat – 0.3 g

Protein – 1.2 g

Calories – 47

Ingredients:

- 1 bunch basil leaves
- 7 limes, quartered
- 3 cups water
- 1 1/4 tsp stevia powdered extract
- 9 ice cubes

Instructions:

1. Place the basil leaves and stevia into a jar and crush together.
2. Juice the limes into the jar. Add the rind to the jar too.
3. Add water.
4. Add crushed ice and cool in the fridge.
5. Serve.

Rosemary Lemonade

Prep time: 15 minutes + 1-2 hours to cool in the fridge

Cooking time: 5 minutes

Servings: 2

Nutrients per serving:

Total Carbs – 8.8 g

Fat – 0.4 g

Protein – 1.1 g

Calories – 29

Ingredients:

- 2 sprigs rosemary
- ½ tsp ginger
- 3 lemons, juice + zest
- 2 cups water
- 12 drops liquid stevia
- Ice, to taste (usually more than half glass covered)

Instructions:

1. In a pan, combine water, lemon peel, and 1 rosemary sprig. Bring to boil. Then boil for 5 min.
2. Remove from heat and filter out the peel and the sprig.
3. Add ginger and let cool.
4. Stir in stevia and lemon juice.
5. Put a rosemary sprig and some lemon slices into a jar and pour the lemonade into it.
6. Cool in the fridge.

Mint Lemonade

Prep time: 1 hour 3 minutes

Cooking time: 3 minutes

Servings: 2

Nutrients per serving:

Total Carbs – 5.7 g

Fat – 0.2 g

Protein – 0.8 g

Calories – 19

Ingredients:

- 2 lemons, juiced
- ½ cup fresh mint leaves, chopped
- 1 tsp stevia, liquid
- 4 cups sparkling water

Instructions:

1. Combine all ingredients and let stand in the fridge for 1 hour.
2. Filter and serve.

Ginger Lemonade

Prep time: 15 minutes

Cooking time: 2 minutes

Servings: 1 cup

Nutrients per serving:

Total Carbs – 16 g

Fat – 2.1 g

Protein – 2.3 g

Calories – 97

Ingredients:

- ½ cup water
- ½ cup lemon juice
- 2-inch piece ginger, peeled, sliced
- 1 tsp liquid stevia
- Sparkling water
- Ice (usually more than half glass covered)

Instructions:

1. In a pot, combine water, sweetener, and ginger. Bring to a boil, and remove from heat and let cool.
2. Add lemon juice.
3. Strain the mixture into a jar and store in the fridge.
4. To serve, take some lemon ginger syrup and mix with sparkling water and ice.

Raspberry Lemonade

Prep time: 2 minutes

Cooking time: 0 minutes

Servings: 3

Nutrients per serving:

Total Carbs – 6.6 g

Fat – 0.9 g

Protein – 1.1 g

Calories – 41

Ingredients:

- 1 cup raspberry
- 1 cup lemon juice
- 3 cups water
- Ice, to taste (usually more than half glass covered)

Instructions:

1. Blend 1 cup raspberry with 3/4 cup water.
2. Strain mixture, keeping only the liquid.
3. Combine raspberry water, lemon juice, water, and ice.

Warm Drinks

Rosehip Drink

Prep time: 45 minutes

Cooking time: 3 minutes

Servings: 5

Nutrients per serving:

Total Carbs – 16 g

Fat – 0.8 g

Protein – 0.5 g

Calories – 69

Ingredients:

- 1 cup dried rosehips, rinsed
- 5 cups water
- 1 lemon, juiced
- 1 tsp stevia

Instructions:

1. In a pan, combine rosehips, water, and stevia. Bring to boil.
2. Cover and let stand for 30 minutes.
3. Strain the mixture, keeping only the liquid, and add the lemon juice.
4. Serve.

Cranberry Non-alcoholic Gluhwein

Prep time: 3 minutes

Cooking time: 17 minutes

Servings: 4

Nutrients per serving:

Total Carbs – 37 g

Fat – 0.3 g

Protein – 0.3 g

Calories – 148

Ingredients:

- 1 tangerine, sliced
- 4 cups cranberry juice
- 2 cinnamon stalks
- 6 cloves
- Dash of nutmeg

Instructions:

1. In a pan, combine the tangerine, spices, and cranberry juice.
2. Let simmer for 5-7 minutes.
3. Remove from heat and let stand for 10 minutes, covered.
4. Serve.

Masala Tea

Prep time: 10 minutes

Cooking time: 10 minutes

Servings: 2

Nutrients per serving:

Total Carbs – 15 g

Fat – 20.4 g

Protein – 0.2 g

Calories – 210

Ingredients:

- 2 cups water
- 2 tsp black tea
- ½ cup heavy cream
- ¼ tsp ginger
- 1 anise star
- 1 cinnamon stick
- 2 cardamom pods
- 2 whole cloves
- Dash of ground pepper
- ½ tsp stevia

Instructions:

1. In a pan, combine the water and 1/4 cup heavy cream.
2. When heated, add black tea and spices.
3. Bring to boil.
4. Stir in remaining cream.
5. Add stevia and cover. Let stand for 2-4 minutes.
6. Serve.

Hot Chocolate

Prep time: 15 minutes

Cooking time: 7 minutes

Servings: 2

Nutrients per serving:

Total Carbs – 0.5 g

Fat – 26.4 g

Protein – 3.5 g

Calories – 263

Ingredients:

- 1 ½ cup water
- 1 oz black bitter chocolate, broken into pieces
- 1 cup heavy cream, low fat
- ¼ tsp cinnamon
- Sweetener, to taste

Instructions:

1. Bring water to boil, reduce heat, and stir in chocolate until it melts.
2. Add cinnamon and sweetener.
3. Add heavy cream, remove from heat, and blend using a blender.

Chicory Coffee

Prep time: 2 minutes

Cooking time: 12 minutes

Servings: 2

Nutrients per serving:

Total Carbs – 8 g

Fat – 18 g

Protein – 2.1 g

Calories – 193

Ingredients:

- 2 Tbsp roasted chicory root
- 2 Tbsp coconut butter
- Dash of nutmeg
- 2 cups water

Instructions:

1. Place the chicory root in a pot and cover with water.
2. Bring to boil, then let simmer for 2 minutes.
3. Remove from the heat and let stand for 5 minutes.
4. Strain and transfer to a blender.
5. Blend with coconut butter and dash of nutmeg.
6. Add sweetener to your coffee if desired and serve.

Cilantro Tea

Prep time: 2 minutes

Cooking time: 15 minutes

Servings: 1

Nutrients per serving:

Total Carbs – 1 g

Fat – 0 g

Protein – 0.5 g

Calories – 5

Ingredients:

- 1 tbsp cilantro seeds / 2 tbsp cilantro leaves
- 1 cup boiling water
- Sweetener, to taste

Instructions:

1. Combine ingredients and let stand, covered, for 15 minutes.
2. Add sweetener and serve.

Schizandra Berry Tea

Prep time: 2 minutes

Cooking time: 15 minutes

Servings: 1

Nutrients per serving:

Total Carbs – 0 g

Fat – 0 g

Protein – 0 g

Calories – 5

Ingredients:

- 10 **S**chizandra berries (Chinese magnolia-vine)
- 1 cup boiling water
- Sweetener, to taste

Instructions:

1. Combine ingredients and let stand, covered, for 15 minutes.
2. Add sweetener and serve.

M & M Tea

Prep time: 2 minutes

Cooking time: 15 minutes

Servings: 2

Nutrients per serving:

Total Carbs – 4.5 g

Fat – 0.4 g

Protein – 1.7 g

Calories – 23

Ingredients:

- 10 mint leaves
- 10 Melissa lemon balm leaves
- 2 cups boiling water
- Lemon slice

Instructions:

1. Combine ingredients and let stand, covered, for 15 minutes.
2. Add lemon slice and serve.

Chamomile & Co Tea

Prep time: 2 minutes

Cooking time: 15 minutes

Servings: 2

Nutrients per serving:

Total Carbs – 0.5 g

Fat – 0.1 g

Protein – 0.1 g

Calories – 2

Ingredients:

- 2 tsp chamomile flowers
- 1 tsp lavender flowers
- 2 cups water
- Lemon slices to serve and to taste

Instructions:

1. Combine ingredients and let stand, covered, for 15 minutes.
2. Add lemon slice and serve.

Citrus Tea

Prep time: 15 minutes

Cooking time: 3 minutes

Servings: 2

Nutrients per serving:

Total Carbs – 4.5 g

Fat – 0.1 g

Protein – 0.4 g

Calories – 17

Ingredients:

- 2 Tbsp hibiscus tea
- 2 lemon slices, peeled
- 3 orange slices, peeled
- 3 grapefruit slices, peeled
- 2 cups water
- Sweetener, to taste

Instructions:

1. In a pan, combine all ingredients and bring to a boil. Let stand, covered, for 3 minutes.
2. Add sweetener and lemon slice to taste and serve.

Sea-buckthorn Tea

Prep time: 15 minutes

Cooking time: 7 minutes

Servings: 2

Nutrients per serving:

Total Carbs – 13 g

Fat – 1.4 g

Protein – 0.5 g

Calories – 29

Ingredients:

- 4 Tbsp sea buckthorn
- 1 tsp grated ginger
- 2 cups water
- 1 stick cinnamon
- 2 stars anise
- Sweetener, to taste

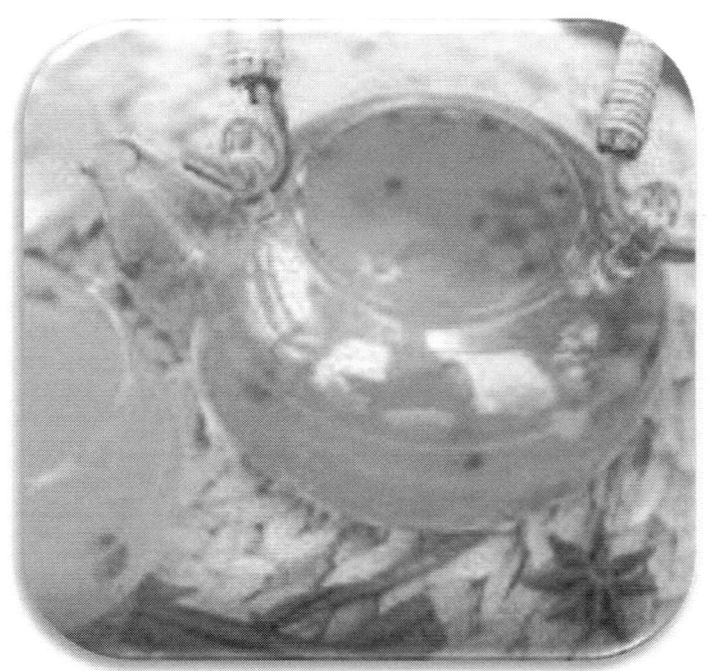

Instructions:

1. In a pot, smash the berries of sea buckthorn with a fork.
2. Add ginger and water and bring to boil.
3. Remove from heat and add cinnamon and anise. Let stand for 7-10 minutes, covered.
4. Serve adding sweetener to taste.

Apple Peel Tea

Prep time: 15 minutes

Cooking time: 15 minutes

Servings: 2

Nutrients per serving:

Total Carbs – 0.5 g

Fat – 0 g

Protein – 0 g

Calories – 1

Ingredients:

- 3 Tbsp apple dried peel or dried apples
- 2 cups water
- ½ stick cinnamon
- Sweetener, to taste

Instructions:

1. In a pot, combine all ingredients, cover, and bring to a boil.
2. Let stand 15 minutes, then serve.

Alcoholic Drinks

Eggnog

Prep time: 4 hours 10 minutes

Cooking time: 10 minutes

Servings: 2

Nutrients per serving:

Total Carbs – 4 g

Fat – 50.7 g

Protein – 8.8 g

Calories – 537

Ingredients:

- 2 egg whites
- 2 egg yolks
- 1 cup heavy cream
- 2 Tbsp sweetener, divided
- 1 tsp vanilla extract
- 1 tsp cinnamon
- ½ tsp nutmeg
- 2 Tbsp brandy

Instructions:

1. Whisk together egg yolks and 1 Tbsp sweetener.
2. Whisk together egg whites and 1 Tbsp sweetener until foamy.
3. Add heavy cream to whisked yolks. Transfer to a pan. Heat until viscous. Remove from heat.
4. Combine whisked egg whites with yolk mixture.
5. Add vanilla extract, cinnamon, nutmeg, and brandy.
6. Refrigerate for 4 hours and serve.

Ginger Vodka

Prep time: 5 minutes

Cooking time: 0 minutes

Servings: 2

Nutrients per serving:

Total Carbs – 3.2 g

Fat – 0.1 g

Protein – 0.2 g

Calories – 46

Ingredients:

- 1.5 oz vodka
- 1 Tbsp fresh ginger, grated finely
- 30 ml lemon juice
- 1 tsp white honey

Instructions:

1. Squeeze the juice out of the grated ginger.
2. Combine vodka, lemon, ginger juice, and honey. Serve.

Berry Champagne

Prep time: 5 minutes

Cooking time: 0 minutes

Servings: 5

Nutrients per serving:

Total Carbs – 5.5 g

Fat – 0.2 g

Protein – 0.4 g

Calories – 25

Ingredients:

- 1 bottle champagne
- 2 cups berries (strawberries or blueberries)
- 3 Tbsp orange juice
- 5 mint sprigs

Instructions:

1. Freeze empty champagne glasses for 20 minutes.
2. Combine berries and juice in a blender and pulse on high.
3. Divide the berry puree between glasses and pour in champagne.
4. Decorate with mint and serve.

Tea & Champagne Cocktail

Prep time: 3 minutes

Cooking time: 0 minutes

Servings: 2

Nutrients per serving:

Total Carbs – 0.5 g

Fat – 0 g

Protein – 0.1 g

Calories – 3

Ingredients:

- 3 tsp black tea
- ½ lemon
- Sweetener, to taste
- 1 cup water
- 2-3 oz champagne, semi-sweet. cooled

Instructions:

1. Brew the tea.
2. Add lemon and sweetener.
3. Chill and filter out tea leaves.
4. Mix tea with champagne and serve.

Blue Lagoon

Prep time: 3 minutes

Cooking time: 0 minutes

Servings: 1

Nutrients per serving:

Total Carbs – 9.5 g

Fat – 0 g

Protein – 0.1 g

Calories – 143

Ingredients:

- 1 oz vodka
- 0.67 oz Blue Curacao
- 2 tsp lemon juice
- 4 oz soda
- Ice

Instructions:

1. Combine all ingredients and serve in a highball glass.

Sangria

Prep time: 1 minute

Cooking time: 0 minutes

Servings: 2

Nutrients per serving:

Total Carbs – 8 g

Fat – 0 g

Protein – 0 g

Calories – 73

Ingredients:

- 3.75 oz red dry wine
- 3.75 oz orange soda
- Crushed ice

Instructions:

1. Add ice at the bottom of a glass and pour in wine and soda.

Vodka Mojito

Prep time: 2 minutes

Cooking time: 0 minutes

Servings: 1

Nutrients per serving:

Total Carbs – 2 g

Fat – 0 g

Protein – 0 g

Calories – 109

Ingredients:

- 1 shot vodka
- 1 splash club soda
- 2 Tbsp lime juice
- ½ tsp granulated stevia
- 4 fresh mint leaves (+more for garnish)
- Ice to taste

Instructions:

1. Smash mint leaves with sweetener and lime juice.
2. Add ice to a glass.
3. Pour in vodka and soda. Garnish with mint leaves.

Chili Mojito

Prep time: 4 hours

Cooking time: 0 minutes

Servings: 1

Nutrients per serving:

Total Carbs – 3 g

Fat – 0 g

Protein – 0 g

Calories – 83

Ingredients:

- 2 oz tequila
- 1 chili, cut in half
- 3.5 oz soda
- 3.5 oz lime juice
- 1 egg white
- 2 tsp salt
- 1 tsp paprika
- 18 fresh mint leaves, torn
- lime wedges for garnish
- Ice

Instructions:

1. Let the chili halves soak in the tequila for 4 hours.
2. Rim the top of 2 glasses with the egg white.
3. Mix together salt and paprika, and sprinkle on the glass rims.
4. Pour in the tequila, lime juice, and ice.
5. Add mint and soda.

Dark 'N' Stormy

Prep time: 2 minutes

Cooking time: 0 minutes

Servings: 1

Nutrients per serving:

Total Carbs – 1.5 g

Fat – 0 g

Protein – 0 g

Calories –

Ingredients:

- 2 oz rum
- ½ lime, juiced
- 4 oz sugar free ginger beer
- Ice

Instructions:

1. Fill a glass with ice.
2. Add rum and squeezed lime. Stir well.
3. Add ginger beer.

Vanilla Old Fashioned

Prep time: 2 minutes

Cooking time: 0 minutes

Servings: 1

Nutrients per serving:

Total Carbs – 0 g

Fat – 0 g

Protein – 0 g

Calories – 131

Ingredients:

- 2 oz bourbon
- 1-2 oz diet soda
- 1-inch piece orange peel
- 1-inch vanilla bean, halved
- ½ Tbsp Torani vanilla syrup
- Ice

Instructions:

1. At the bottom of a glass, muddle orange peel with vanilla bean.
2. Pour in bourbon and vanilla syrup.
3. Stir and add ice.
4. Add in soda.

Tom Collins

Prep time: 2 minutes

Cooking time: 15 minutes

Servings: 1

Nutrients per serving:

Total Carbs – 2 g

Fat – 0 g

Protein – 9 g

Calories – 117

Ingredients:

- 3 oz gin
- 1-2 oz diet soda
- 2 oz lemon juice
- 1 cup water
- 1 cup erythritol
- Lemon/lime slices
- 1 cup ice

Instructions:

1. Prepare sweet syrup by bringing water and erythritol to a boil.
2. Cool the syrup.
3. Add gin, lemon juice, syrup, and 1 cup ice to a shaker.
4. Shake well and strain into a glass. Add soda.
5. Serve with lime slice.

Red Dog

Prep time: 1 minute

Cooking time: 0 minutes

Servings: 1

Nutrients per serving:

Total Carbs – 16 g

Fat – 0.1 g

Protein – 0.4 g

Calories – 118

Ingredients:

- 0.8 oz tequila
- 0.8 oz Sambuca
- 2 ml Tabasco sauce

Instructions:

1. Pour Sambuca in a shot glass.
2. Using a bar spoon, pour in tequila so it doesn't combine with Sambuca.
3. Add tabasco by the drop and serve.

Wasabi Margarita

Prep time: 1 minute

Cooking time: 0 minutes

Servings: 1

Nutrients per serving:

Total Carbs – 0.8 g

Fat – 0.5 g

Protein – 0.2 g

Calories – 210

Ingredients:

- 1.6 oz tequila Silver
- 1.6 oz orange liqueur
- 1 tsp wasabi
- 1 ½ Tbsp lemon juice
- Ice

Instructions:

1. Combine all ingredients and shake well in a shaker.
2. Serve in a glass rimmed with salt.

Black Russian

Prep time: 1 minute

Cooking time: 0 minutes

Servings: 1

Nutrients per serving:

Total Carbs – 9.5 g

Fat – 0.1 g

Protein – 0 g

Calories – 199

Ingredients:

- 1.6 oz vodka
- 0.8 oz coffee liqueur
- Ice cubes

Instructions:

1. Fill a glass with ice cubes.
2. Pour in vodka and coffee liqueur and mix with a cocktail spoon.

White Russian

Prep time: 1 minute

Cooking time: 0 minutes

Servings: 1

Nutrients per serving:

Total Carbs – 12 g

Fat – 1.1 g

Protein – 0 g

Calories – 189

Ingredients:

- 1 oz vodka
- 1 oz coffee liqueur
- 1 oz low fat cream
- Ice cubes

Instructions:

1. Fill the glass with ice cubes.
2. Add in cream, coffee liqueur, and vodka. Mix with a cocktail spoon.

Rum Cucumber

Prep time: 15 minute

Cooking time: 2 minutes

Servings: 2

Nutrients per serving:

Total Carbs – 17 g

Fat – 0.6 g

Protein – 1.8 g

Calories – 100

Ingredients:

- 2 oz white rum
- 2 cucumbers, juiced
- 1 oz ginger lime syrup (4 tbsp grated ginger + 1 cup lime juice + 1 cup sweetener)
- 2 oz club soda
- Ice

Instructions:

1. Prepare the syrup: bring lime juice, sweetener, and ginger to a boil. Simmer for 3 minutes and remove from heat. Let cool and strain. Place in the fridge.
2. Add rum, lime syrup, and cucumber juice to a cocktail shaker with some ice. Shake well and pour in a glass.
3. Top with club soda.

CONCLUSION

Thank you for reading this book and having the patience to try the recipes.

I do hope that you gain as much enjoyment reading and experimenting with the meals as I have had writing this book.

If you would like to leave a comment, you can do it at the Order section->Digital orders, in your amazon account.

Stay safe and healthy!

Recipe Index

Conversion Tables

VALUE EQUIVALENTS (LIQUID)

US STANDARD	US STANDARD (OUNCES)	METRIC (VOLUME)
2 tablespoons	1 fl. oz.	30 mL
¼ cup	2 fl. oz.	60 mL
½ cup	4 fl. oz.	120 mL
1 cup	8 fl. oz.	240mL
1 ½ cup	12 fl. oz.	355 mL
2 cups or 1 pint	16 fl. oz.	`475 mL
4 cups or 1 quart	32 fl. oz.	1 L
1 gallon	128 fl. oz.	4 L

OVEN TEMPERATURES

FAHRENHEIT(F)	CELSIUS(C) APPROXIMATE
250 °F	120 °C
300 °F	150 °C
325 °F	165 °C
350 °F	180 °C
375 °F	190°C
400 °F	200 °C
425 °F	220 °C
450 °F	230 °C

VALUE EQUIVALENTS (LIQUID)

US STANDARD	METRIC (APPROXIMATE)
$\frac{1}{8}$ teaspoon	0.5 mL
¼ teaspoon	1 mL
½ teaspoon	2 mL
$\frac{2}{3}$ teaspoon	4 mL
1 teaspoon	5 mL
1 tablespoon	15 mL
¼ cup	59 mL
$\frac{1}{3}$ cup	79 mL
½ cup	118 mL
$\frac{2}{3}$ cup	156 mL
¾ cup	177 mL
1 cup	235 mL
2 cups or 1 pint	475 mL
3 cups	700 mL
4 cups or 1 quart	1 L
½ gallon	2 L
1 gallon	4 L

WEIGHT EQUIVALENTS

US STANDARD	METRIC (APPROXIMATE)
½ ounce	15 g
1 ounces	30 g
2 ounces	60 g
4 ounces	115 g
8 ounces	225 g
12 ounces	340 g
16 ounce or 1 pound	455 g

Other Books by Emma Green

Emma Green's page on Amazon

https://goo.gl/7yn2fR

Manufactured by Amazon.ca
Bolton, ON